ROUTLEDGE LIBRARY EDITIONS:
EDUCATION

EDUCATION IN THE SECONDARY MODERN SCHOOL

EDUCATION IN THE SECONDARY MODERN SCHOOL

J. J. B. DEMPSTER

Volume 94

LONDON AND NEW YORK

First published in 1946

This edition first published in 2012
by Routledge
2 Park Square, Milton Park, Abingdon, Oxfordshire OX14 4RN

Simultaneously published in the USA and Canada
by Routledge
711 Third Avenue, New York, NY 10017

First issued in paperback 2014

Routledge is an imprint of the Taylor and Francis Group, an informa company

© 1946 J. J. B. Dempster

All rights reserved. No part of this book may be reprinted or reproduced or utilised in any form or by any electronic, mechanical, or other means, now known or hereafter invented, including photocopying and recording, or in any information storage or retrieval system, without permission in writing from the publishers.

Trademark notice: Product or corporate names may be trademarks or registered trademarks, and are used only for identification and explanation without intent to infringe.

British Library Cataloguing in Publication Data
A catalogue record for this book is available from the British Library

ISBN 13: 978-0-415-68910-6 (Volume 94)
ISBN 13: 978-0-415-75080-6 (pbk)

Publisher's Note
The publisher has gone to great lengths to ensure the quality of this reprint but points out that some imperfections in the original copies may be apparent.

Disclaimer
The publisher has made every effort to trace copyright holders and would welcome correspondence from those they have been unable to trace.

EDUCATION IN THE SECONDARY MODERN SCHOOL

By

J. J. B. DEMPSTER, M.A.

With a Foreword by
SIR FRED CLARKE

LONDON
THE PILOT PRESS LTD
1947

*First published in 1946, by The
Pilot Press, Ltd., 45 Great Russell
Street, London, W.C.1
Reprinted* 1947.

PRINTED AND BOUND IN GREAT BRITAIN BY
W. & J. MACKAY AND CO., LTD., CHATHAM.

CONTENTS

I. THE MODERN SCHOOL CHILD 9

II. TEACHING THE BASIC SKILLS 14
    (*a*) ARITHMETIC
    (*b*) READING

III. THE FUNCTION OF PRACTICAL WORK 24

IV. ART, MUSIC, DRAMA AND PHYSICAL EDUCATION .. 29

V. THE SOCIAL STUDIES 35

VI. THE DEVELOPMENT OF PROJECTS 41

VII. SCIENCE, AND THE SCIENTIFIC ATTITUDE 53

VIII. PROBLEMS OF GRADING AND SPECIALISATION .. 59

IX. TEACHERS' PROBLEMS 65

X. THE EXTRA YEAR, AND THE SPIRIT OF THE SCHOOL 71

FOREWORD

I AM glad and honoured to have this opportunity of contributing a Foreword to these chapters by my friend and former student, Mr. J. J. B. Dempster.

I was myself so impressed by the value and timeliness of the original articles as they appeared in the *Schoolmaster* that I took them out and preserved them on file. No doubt many other readers will have done the same so it is gratifying to know that the work is now to appear in book form.

It is impossible to exaggerate the importance of the educational field that Mr. Dempster is exploring. We may hope not only that many others will follow his example but also that some wide concerted attacks on the problems may be organised, involving the co-operation of many skilled investigators in a wide diversity of circumstances.

Fears as well as hopes stir in the mind as one contemplates the task that is set us by those provisions of the Education Act which inaugurate, at long last, the era of Secondary Education For All. We may fail to take the just measure of the sheer magnitude of the undertaking. Still more probably, and perhaps even more disastrously, we may underestimate its unfamiliar *novelty* for a people whose educational history has trained them to think of secondary education in very different terms.

One way of obscuring the novelty of the task and of implying that the old ways are capable of meeting the new needs is to play down the forthright definition of secondary education that appears in the Act—" education suitable to the requirements of senior pupils "—and instead to concentrate on specific " types " of secondary school. By such means we conceal from ourselves the true nature and extent of the task before us, which is nothing less than a complete and comprehensive re-consideration of the education of the adolescent over the whole range. To think primarily and mainly in terms of pre-ordained " types " is to study the real problem through distorting media. It is so easy, almost without realising it, to drop into the way of assuming that the grammar school just stays put and that technical secondary and modern secondary are just old " junior technical " and " senior elementary " written a little longer. A curious threefold squint is thus substituted for direct vision of the actual problem in all its magnitude and novelty.

True, we must start the new order with what the old order has left us. That is obvious enough ; we cannot suspend all schooling for five years or more while we bring into being a brand new system. The danger arises only when we assume that what we start with is what we are looking for, and so fail to realise that we do not know the answers and that the situation calls for adventurous experiment all along the line and in every type of school.

Of all the types the least trammelled by precedent and the least likely to be deflected by extraneous influences is the so-called secondary " modern " school. It is well fitted to be the pioneer in the bold and enterprising experiment in which, sooner or later, all alike will have to take part.

What I am concerned to insist upon is that in so taking the lead the " modern " school will be doing much more than shaping its own immediate destiny. It will also be arriving at results which, in due measure, will have relevance and validity over the whole range of secondary education. For it is to be feared that the secondary school as we have known it, great as its achievements have been, does need the stimulus of a fresh approach to immediate realities as they should be apprehended by the growing youth.

Mr. Dempster is well qualified by long experience and by prolonged study to apply just this stimulus. Directness of approach and concreteness of treatment are outstanding features of his proposals for the work of the " modern " school. So I can very gladly commend his book to those, and they are many, who are anxiously seeking for the right lines of experiment and advance.

In so doing I would again express the hope that others will

follow his example and help to build up that body of reconsidered knowledge concerning " education suitable to the requirements of senior pupils," of which we now stand in such need.

F. CLARKE.

ACKNOWLEDGMENT

The material in this book first appeared during the Autumn of 1945 and Spring of 1946 as a series of articles in *The Schoolmaster*, and it is now republished by permission of the Editor, to whom I acknowledge my grateful thanks. In putting this material into book form I have revised and brought it up-to-date, and have expanded those parts where further explanation appeared to be needed.

J. J. B. DEMPSTER.

CHAPTER 1

THE MODERN SCHOOL CHILD

THE problem of the Secondary Modern School is one of the most pressing that face education at the moment. Although no figure was stated in the Education Act of 1944, it looks as though some 70 per cent of the children of the Primary School will find their way either into the Secondary Modern School or into similar classes in a Multilateral School. That is, seven out of each ten future voters and citizens will prepare for these functions in schools whose aims and curricula lack that foundation of tradition and practice upon which the future of Secondary Grammar and Technical Schools can be developed.

The Grammar School looks to the University for its guide; the Secondary Technical School looks to the Technical College; but the Modern School has no guide of this sort. Yet the Modern School shares with its fellow Secondary Schools the overriding aim of preparing its pupils for life, and, after all, that is what really matters. The fact that those who direct the Modern School need to keep this aim foremost in their minds may eventually bring their school to greater heights of achievement than we are able to forecast at the moment.

Milton said : " I call a complete and generous education that which fits a man to perform justly, skilfully and magnanimously all the offices, both public and private, of both peace and war." In a democracy every citizen must play his part, so this applies with equal stress to all types of schools. In Plato's republic, or in a totalitarian state where everything is cut and dried, it is presumably possible that the destiny of each child can be so exactly foreseen that he can be drilled in detail to fulfil it ; but in a democracy, " Education is not learning what to do, but becoming the kind of person who knows what to do." In other words, the educator is not training a robot but is enabling each child to achieve his full personal and social maturity both for his own benefit and as his contribution to a world in which he lives.

THE CHILDREN'S ATTITUDE

What are the children like who come to the Modern School? Let us remember that they form some 70 per cent of their age group and thus cannot all be classed as " dull and backward." Some of them will be, but two out of every seven will be above the average in intelligence and attainments, while the majority will be packed around the " average." It is false to look upon Modern School children as " duds," yet a great many of the children who come to the Modern Schools today regard themselves in this light. In their Primary Schools they have been prepared for a competitive scholarship examination and they have failed. A good Primary School may have mitigated this to some extent, and the gradual abandonment of the competitive examination may alleviate it in the future, but the fact remains that many of the children who pass to the Modern School today look upon themselves as rejects, a view which only too often they see to be shared by their parents. Linked to this is a general turning from books and a dislike for academic subjects, for their failure has been in these. For this reason one of the first aims of a Modern School must be to study each individual pupil carefully and plan ways and means to rebuild his self-respect.

Another difficulty faced by teachers of these children is their apparent lack of interest. It is necessary to seek the reason for this. Very young children are dependent upon their elders, but gradually, as their knowledge of the world around them increases, they attain a mastery of it that gives them the stability and assurance so characteristic of the upper part of the Primary School. They are keenly interested in people and things and their unbounded curiosity shows itself in untiring questioning about all and sundry. This curiosity in things is gradually replaced during early adolescence by interest in ideas and ideals, but the change takes place slowly. Among the more intelligent children the transition is made by a change of emphasis within the academic subjects, but the Modern School child lacks this bridge. Moreover, it seems that less intelligent children, and especially those with a less helpful home environment, make the transition more slowly or do not make it at all. The raising of the school leaving age may enable more of them to complete the change during their school life, but the fact remains that many of them today, especially in the upper part of the school, are not interested in anything. They have left behind them the forceful curiosity of the Primary School and have not yet acquired the more abstract questioning Spirit of thoughtful adolescence.

RESULTS OF CHILD STUDY

The problem of educating these children has to be considered against a background of our present-day knowledge of psychology. First let us clear away some misconceptions. The old idea that a teacher could develop his pupil's " faculties " of memory, observation and the like by exercising them with studies suited to this purpose has gone by the board. So has the conception of a child as a machine which responds and develops to certain stimuli as steadily and regularly as any other piece of mechanism. Gone, too, is the idea that children have an equal capacity for assimilating knowledge, and that the teachers err if all their children do not attain the same standard in their work. More recently opinion has swung away from those exaggerated forms of " free discipline " and " soft pedagogy " which were symbols of the reaction against formalism and the various mechanistic conceptions.

All these ideas have been either abandoned by psychologists or so fundamentally modified that they can scarcely be recognised. This is no mere matter of changing fashions in psychology; there is an ever growing corpus of theory that has now been tested widely and thoroughly in school conditions and upon which educational psychologists are agreed. There are still many fields in which they disagree, but the framework of a fundamentally sound psychology of education is beginning to appear. The science of psychology has made such rapid strides in the last few decades that practising teachers find it difficult to keep pace with it, and thus discredited theories still persist in many schools, and educational practices suffer in consequence.

What is the position today? It is recognised that there are wide variations in the general capacities of children and certain differences in their ability patterns; this stresses the need for an individual approach. The psychologist no longer regards the child as a mechanism, but as an organism; this implies a demand on the child to reach out for what education offers, rather than an emphasis upon the efforts of the teacher to force or wheedle education into a malleable pupil. It is realised that the mere learning and retention of facts is valueless unless this leads to concepts and attitudes, and that these can only be developed by the child's own efforts and incorporated in his developing self. Children are not looked upon as bundles of disparate characteristics, but as beings with intricate and interdependent behaviour patterns who must be considered as persons within whom harmonious development is necessary if an integrated personality is to be achieved.

Lastly, the individual is not regarded as an individual alone, but as a member of the society in which he moves, so his social education is as important as his personal education.

To sum up, the child is an individual of varying abilities who, by his own efforts, acquires concepts and develops emotions which, if properly balanced, will enable him to mature as an individual and take his rightful place among his fellows to their mutual advantage. Every phrase in this description holds implications which it will be necessary to recall as we consider in more practical detail the problems of the Modern School.

BOOK LIST

There may be some who would wish to study the principles outlined above more fully and for them a brief note of a few recent books are given below. If I had to choose two only of these books, I should read Fleming and Stead, but I would have Pinsent by me for reference.

Fundamentals of Democratic Education, by Robert Ulich ; The American Book Co., 1940. A detailed philosophical discussion of the function of education in a democratic society. Rather heavy reading but full of good things.

The Education of a Community, by H. G. Stead ; University of London Press, 1942. A readable and stimulating book dealing directly with the educational problems which confront us today.

Conflicting Psychologies of Learning, by Boyd Henry Bode ; D. C. Heath and Co., 1929. A clear and straightforward account of the historical development of the theory of learning. Does not come down to the present.

Basic Principles of Education, by Henry C. Morrison ; Harrap, 1933. An excellent account of education as adjustment, but neglects other aspects of the subject. Valuable for its picture of the individual and his needs.

The Principles of Teaching Method, by A. Pinsent ; Harrap, 1941. A most important account of the psychological foundation of modern teaching method, so crammed with close reasoning that it is easier to use as a reference book than for straight reading.

The Social Psychology of Education, by C. M. Fleming ; Kegan Paul, 1944. A very readable and fully documented account of the psychological background of the school. From the point of view of what we have discussed above, the most valuable book in this list.

CHAPTER II

Teaching the Basic Skills

NOBODY can pull his weight in modern society unless he has mastered the simple educational tools of Reading, Writing and Arithmetic. Since these are so fundamental in all school work it will be helpful to consider them fully before we turn to other aspects of the Modern School.

It is most helpful when children come to the Modern School from Primary Schools with complete records of their attainments. Where this is not the case, much time will be saved, and a clearer picture of the problem of each child be obtained, if their attainments and potentialities are fully examined by means of standardised tests as soon as the children enter the Modern School.

An Intelligence Test, which will give us some idea of the potentiality of each child in terms of I.Q. and mental age, is of prime importance. Some of the children will be poor readers, so the Intelligence Test should be prefaced by a simple Reading Test to decide what type of Intelligence Test will be most suitable.

The Intelligence Test can be followed by an Arithmetic Test which gives an Arithmetic Quotient similar to the Intelligence Quotient, or an Arithmetical Age similar to the Mental Age. By means of these we can divide the children into three groups. There will be those of reasonably high mental ability whose arithmetical attainment is also high; we shall discuss their future later. A second group will be reasonably intelligent, but will lag behind this in their arithmetical attainment; these are the retarded children who need special help. Lastly, there will be those whose intelligence and arithmetical attainment are both low, and these need treatment too specialised to be discussed in this short book.

A. ARITHMETIC

It is well to pause here a moment and ask ourselves just how much mechanical arithmetic adults need in their everyday life. That is, what is the essential minimum which every child should master if he can?

Multiplication Tables	Simple Fractions
Common Weights and Measures	Simple Decimals
The Four Rules, simple and compound	Simple Percentages
	Simple Mensuration

It is easy enough to pile on these much more on one plea or another until our " minimum " becomes a maximum, but we must cut drastically and keep to essentials. Notice that fractions, decimals, percentages and mensuration are introduced on the practical level only. In the four rules, the biggest problem is that of the " long " forms of multiplication and division, especially the compound.

There have been many investigations recently into the age at which the various arithmetical processes can best be introduced, and it has been generally agreed that we tend to bring in the more difficult rules far too early. It is better to wait a year or two and then sail through a new rule than to introduce it too soon and flounder for lesson after lesson. Thus it is suggested that compound long multiplication and division at any rate should be left until the third year in the school, and that there should be no hurry to press on with other rules if individuals or groups of children find them difficult.

REMEDIAL WORK

In order to help the middle group of children, those whose arithmetical attainment is less than their intelligence would lead us to expect, we must locate the weak spots of each individual. Schonell, in the *Diagnosis of Individual Difficulties in Arithmetic* (Oliver and Boyd), describes how this can be done, and he has produced a set of Diagnostic Arithmetic Tests that are more detailed than we need. Using his " *Diagnosis* " it is comparatively simple for a teacher to construct a series of tests, first in tables and then in various rules, which will indicate just where the gaps lie. From a consideration of the results of these, we can show each child exactly what he has to do, and remedial work can begin. Certain of the failures will be common to many, and thus class teaching will be possible, but on the whole the individual approach is better. The child now knows where he stands and therefore takes a personal interest in filling in the gaps and making good his own foundation.

It is useful in this connection to have a series of " target tests " at which the child can aim. These tests should be suited to his stage of arithmetical development and sufficiently thorough for us to be able to say that the child who has passed them has mastered the step tested. There are many arithmetic textbooks which can be adapted for individual work, Nisbet's *New Realistic Arithmetics* being one of the best. At the moment I know of only one arithmetical series in this country which has been scientifically planned and prepared for individual work and that is the *Beacon Arithmetic* published by Ginn. This series is primarily intended for Juniors, but is well adapted to our present purpose. Most of the children in this group will respond rapidly to such treatment as this, but where individuals do not, a more complete study of their difficulties, which should include a consideration of emotional attitude, is needed ; then the scheme can be modified to suit them.

POINTS OF ATTACK

Remedial treatment may also be needed for the upper group of intelligent children with satisfactory arithmetical attainments. When their foundations are secure how shall arithmetical teaching proceed ?

There is a rapidly growing change of emphasis in this subject. At one time textbooks were full of mechanical sums and the problems themselves were almost as mechanical. Then there came the closer application of arithmetic to everyday life. Now the stress is moving even further in this direction and arithmetic in the Modern School is beginning to be regarded as an " informational " subject. Thus, whereas information has been introduced as a pretext for problems, the present tendency is for the problems to take second place to the information. Such an attitude does not detract from the arithmetical value of the work, for it develops the ability to see meaning in number and fully to understand reckoning processes. The study of such matters as shopkeeping, the development of transport (carrying capacity and speed), investments, rates and taxes, the making of plans and maps, deep-sea diving, all have their arithmetical side and can lead to purposeful mental and written activity.

There should be a good deal of practical work in the Modern School, which will be considered in more detail later, but it is worth emphasising here that teachers of practical subjects such as woodwork, metalwork and domestic science should not expect to have a fund of arithmetical knowledge upon which to draw, but should take their very important place as teachers of arithmetic themselves, co-ordinating their work carefully with those who teach arithmetic in the classroom.

Projects in the Modern School will be discussed later. These will provide many situations in which children are faced with the need to use their arithmetical knowledge and each should be fully exploited.

Thus there are at least four points of attack upon arithmetic in Modern Schools. First the child must have a sound mechanical background; remedial treatment on individual lines is needed to achieve this, and it must be realised that the harder rules may with advantage be postponed. Second, the basis of problem work should be informational, the problems forming an adjunct to the information. Third, full use must be made of practical work, the fact that craft teachers are also teachers of arithmetic being fully appreciated. Lastly, projects provide opportunities for children to encounter real situations in which they can use their arithmetical skill.

SUITABLE TESTS

A number of tests have been published which could be used in the manner suggested above but it is important that those selected should be suited to the ages of the children being tested and the ends we have in mind. For this reason one or two tried and reliable tests are given here.

Intelligence Tests, sometimes called Mental Ability Tests, can be classified as either tests using non-verbal items and therefore suitable for non-readers, and tests using verbal items and thus suitable only for children who can read. To decide whether to give a verbal or non-verbal type of Intelligence Test, if the teacher does not know the children well, it is best to give first a simple test of reading comprehension. Schonell's Test R.4 described in his *Backwardness in the Basic Subjects* (Oliver and Boyd), and published separately, is as good as any. If the result of this test shows that the child has a reading age of nine years or less, he should be treated as a non-reader and given a non-verbal type of Intelligence Test.

For children of this age, Jenkins' *Non-Verbal Test of Mental Ability* (published by the National Foundation of Educational Research), is suggested for the non-readers while any of the *Moray House Tests of Mental Ability* (published by the University of London Press) could be used for the children who can read. Moray House also produces Arithmetical Tests which give a reliable assessment of arithmetical attainment.

The standard scores both from the Intelligence Tests suggested here and the Arithmetical Tests are directly comparable, so that it is a simple matter to classify children through them.

	Intelligence	Arithmetic
John Smith	120	118
Peter Jones	80	84
Albert James	110	80

Three different results are shown here. In the first the child is well above average (100) in intelligence and in his attainment in arithmetic. In the second the child is dull, and clearly he is doing as well as can be expected in arithmetic. In the third it is clear that the child is intelligent and should be doing better in his arithmetic than he is. This is the sort of child we should be able to help.

B. READING

Some ten years ago, as part of a fight against juvenile delinquency in Washington, experiments in methods of helping backward readers were carried on in the higher grades of the city's schools. This point of view, that failure to achieve a mastery of reading sets up deep-seated emotional stresses which may have serious results upon the child in school and in his later life, is one that is shared by all experienced teachers of seniors. The danger is realised, but the problem is one of the most difficult that the Modern School has to solve and solution is not always achieved. Today there is more chance of success than there ever was, for the last few years have seen the production of two much needed books on the subject by Professor Schonell, *Backwardness in the Basic Subjects* (1942) and *The Psychology and Teaching of Reading* (1945). What is at least of equal importance, a number of textbooks specially written for the teaching of remedial reading in Senior Schools have been published. These will be described more fully later.

In the previous section we saw that it was necessary before tackling remedial arithmetic to test our pupils so that their present attainments and their potentialities could be ascertained. It was suggested that a reading test such as Schonell's Test R.4 would give a reading age, and that a verbal or non-verbal Intelligence Test would then give an idea of each child's mental potentialities. The two estimates obtained from these tests can now be used to group our pupils into three groups for Reading. Once more those with a low reading age and a low mental age will be omitted from this discussion, since they come under the heading " dull and backward," and need special treatment. The upper group, with high intelligence and a high reading age, only need opportunities, such as a good library and encouragement, to keep them on the right road. The real problem comes from those whose mental age exceeds their reading age ; these are the retarded readers who need, and must have, our help.

REMEDIAL READING

Children reaching the Modern School have been learning to read for five or six years, and those who have failed to achieve a reasonable proficiency will be disheartened and frustrated. It is therefore necessary to make a clean break with the old methods and start the study again from a new angle. During the war the Army Education Corps had to tackle the problem of the small percentage of illiterates in the Army. Some of these men had been gypsies or barge-children who had evaded school; many of them, however, had attended school but had been such poor readers that after leaving they had given up the effort to read. Some of these men had acquired a sense of inferiority which was not easily overcome. But the main point of interest to us is that the A.E.C. produced for them some texts in which the English was very simple but with a content suited to their mature interests, rather on the lines of, " They are open! Come on, Bill, let us go in and have one. Mine is a pint. What is yours?"

At a different level of maturity the same problem is present in the Secondary Modern School, but in this case the level must be that of the child of 11 or 12 and not that of the adult. Approach is the key to the situation; we must overcome the emotional difficulty by doing all in our power to minimise the risk of failure, and we must choose methods and topics suited to the child.

One way of doing this is described by W. V. Warmington in the *New Vista Readers* (Schofield and Sims). He describes four main steps. A picture is discussed and, when the children's interest has been aroused, the teacher, by his questions, obtains from the children sentences which will later appear in the text, and writes them on the blackboard. The children read these sentences and the first step, and usually the first lesson, ends. The children then copy the sentences. The book is not used until the third step comes and by this time the work is familiar and thus the children read with very little difficulty. The last stage is the follow-up, during which the child may draw and label pictures, answer questions, or do some similar work. The scheme is clearly based upon the sentence method, which works well with senior pupils if it is carefully handled. " Look and say " is not omitted, as the labelling of pictures show, but phonetics are relegated to a functional position, being introduced only when there is a real need for them and not as a fundamental basis upon which the teaching is developed.

To progress satisfactorily these children need to work in groups as small and homogeneous as circumstances will allow, if possible having two short reading lessons a day. The teacher's interest in individuals is vital, especially at first, but later group work can play an important part. From the beginning the teacher must be quick to notice any child who is failing to achieve mastery. As a first solution it may be possible to move him to a slower group, but if this fails the child must be tested in more detail to find the reason. Schonell gives tests which can be used for this purpose but, where these fail, the child probably needs psychological guidance and therapeutic treatment.

In choosing material for remedial reading it is important to look for certain points. The subjects must be interesting to the children, and, since pictures can play such an important part in presentation, the illustrations must be clear and pleasing ; the vocabulary must be controlled, that is, new words must not be introduced at random but gradually and methodically ; illustrations and printing must be well set out on the page, not muddled or difficult to see ; and the book must ask children to do things beside read the stories. Some of the books listed below conform to all of these requirements, others to some of them only, but all are written for retarded seniors.

TEXTS FOR RETARDED SENIORS

The New Vista Readers (Schofield and Sims). *The Teacher's Companion* to those quoted above is most useful.
The Speedwell Book (Cassell).
Read, Laugh and Learn (Grant).

The First School Story Book (Nelson).
The First English Work Book (Nelson).
The Active Readers (Ginn).
A Book of Interests (Nisbet).
The New Foundation Readers (University of London Press).

There is a valuable handbook *Reading in Senior Schools*, with the last mentioned series.

ENGLISH A FUNCTIONAL SUBJECT

Reading for the upper group can be most satisfactorily considered when we think of the English as a whole in the Modern School. Reading is primarily important from the comprehension angle, just as the study of English can be summed up in the word " Expression." Both of these concepts imply purpose, and purpose is the key to the teaching of English to these children. Purpose comes from doing something which seems worth while to the children ; to them " studying English " is not necessarily a worthy purpose. Thus much of the English work in the Modern School should be introduced functionally ; that is to say, it should arise naturally as a part of some activity in which the children are engaged. Books should need to be read for information that is required, letters and reports should have to be written for some specific purpose, explanations should have to be given, incidents described and arguments expounded to carry forward some need the children feel to be real and vital.

Of these three divisions, reading, written expression and oral expression, the last is basically important and yet often neglected. All these will find ample place in the project work to be discussed later, and therefore projects can take some of the time usually allotted to formal English work. Not that there should be no formal work. At times both children and teacher feel the need for a study of some particular point over which there is a general difficulty, but this is infrequent. On the other hand, both Writing and Spelling need regular formal attention. A brief period of careful writing can be fitted into every day's work. It need be only five minutes a day, and the spelling need take very little longer. For writing there are many useful copy cards, such as those published by Blackie. For Spelling there are two approaches ; by means of carefully drawn up lists such as Schonell's *A Spelling List for Seniors* (Oliver and Boyd), or, better still, his *Essentials in Teaching and Testing Spelling* (Macmillan), which gives an excellent scheme of testing and a light daily dose of spelling ; or the approach can be made through the child's own errors. A judicious mixture of both is the best, but care must be taken that the second method is not used too fully and the poor speller overwhelmed by his task.

The most important thing to remember is that once reading has been mastered, English is a tool to be used, not a subject to be learned. This point of view must be stressed if the children are to be keen, and therefore to make progress.

The reader may wonder what lies behind the constant references to Schonell. Nothing more than this : nobody has done more in the last few years to help to provide teachers with the tools they need to do their work better, and if we can apply such tools as these to our individual problems with sufficient skill we shall go a long way towards solving the problem of the teaching of the basic subjects.

CHAPTER III

THE FUNCTION OF PRACTICAL WORK

THE value of the practical approach in the Modern School is generally acknowledged, yet the full exploitation of this principle is often hampered by a failure to understand the factors upon which this value depends.

It is a basic principle of teaching that we should proceed from the concrete to the abstract. This is the foundation of modern Infant School technique and its success in that sphere is amply proved. As children grow, their ability to manage without concrete aids develops, and it would seen that this ability is closely linked to what we usually understand when we speak of intelligence. Thus by the time children have reached the age of 12 some of them, the more intelligent, will be able to handle abstractions more easily than others. It is these others, the less intelligent, who enter the Modern Schools at a stage in their development at which the practical approach is still of paramount importance to them.

Not only is this approach suitable to the stage of psychological development of many Modern School entrants, but the stage of their physical development offers new opportunities for practical work. Thus the boy is now ready to handle woodworking tools, and the girl to manage more competently the apparatus of the housewife. The fact that new avenues in education open themselves at this time is especially important to the Modern School child. We discussed in the first chapter the feeling of frustration set up in many children by their failure to pass into the Grammar or Technical Schools, and their consequent turning from academic subjects. The new practical subjects have not the same disadvantages, so the children attack them with less emotional restraint. For this reason there are some who urge us to base the curriculum of the Modern School entirely upon the practical subjects, but, even though we may not go to the lengths these folk would wish, it will be helpful to see how practical work can be broadened and deepened so that the benefits derived from the new method of attack can be extended to all parts of the curriculum.

THE PRACTICAL BASIS

The first requisite is that practical work shall not be treated as a water-tight item in the time-table. Each practical subject, whatever it may be, has its own content, but the aims of those teaching it must extend beyond the content of the subject itself. When speaking of the teaching of arithmetic I drew attention to the importance of the handicraft teacher looking upon himself as a teacher of arithmetic also, and not merely complaining because the arithmetic he needs has not been taught in the classroom. This goes further than suggesting that the handicraft teacher should be also a teacher of arithmetic; it implies that he should be prepared to contribute to the teaching of arithmetic through the medium of his practical subject. Such a principle raises the problem of the position of a handicraft teacher as a specialist who teaches nothing else. It is the old problem of either concentrating upon teaching John a subject, or of teaching John. The question of specialisation in the Modern School will be discussed more fully later. Here it is enough to say that, since the practical approach to education is so profitable to these children, the wider aspect of our practical subjects must be stressed.

Then again, since success in such subjects can be so important in moulding the general emotional attitude of the child to the whole curriculum of his new school, the work must be planned in such a way that he can succeed. It must be carefully adapted to his capabilities. Recent research has proved that in most cases there is a close relationship between a child's ability to succeed in academic work and his ability to produce skilled craft work.

Since intelligence is average or low in the Modern School it would be unwise to set too high a standard for practical work. This does not mean that slipshod work will do. Far from it, for one of the main functions of all schools at all times is to develop in the child a sense of values, to make him appreciate what is good and deprecate the worthless. For this reason it is all the more important that processes should be chosen which the child can master, thus concentrating with a high prospect of success upon a satisfactory finished product. This is already recognised in the planning of courses, but unfortunately many of these are conceived and carried through as though all children could go at the same pace and reach the same goal. There should be more scope for individual differences, so that children can progress at their own speed, the main criterion being that each child shall be able to achieve success as shown by a product of high standard at each stage.

Linked with over-specialisation in practical subjects is the narrow manner in which such subjects are often treated. No practical subject should be treated *in vacuo*. Woodwork and metalwork should reach out and around to include some of the scientific facts they employ, and the children should know more of the origin of the materials they handle and the history of the crafts they follow. It is easy to see how this idea can be extended to the other practical subjects. Needlework leads naturally to a study of the manufacture of textiles, of the production of the fibres and of the lives of the people who produce them ; also to the history of costume. The making of pottery can be based upon its history and the place it has taken as a recorder of history. Weaving offers similar opportunities for expansion. All crafts can lead to simple discussions upon economic topics.

UTILITARIAN AND VOCATIONAL APPEAL

Practical work has yet another appeal to children, especially as they reach the upper parts of the school. It is utilitarian. All the children are potential housewives and potential handymen, so they feel the importance of anything which will be of use to them in later life. Much of our practical work already serves this purpose, but still more could be done. In Domestic Science and Needlework the need is usually met, but in Woodwork and Metalwork boys are more likely to need to effect minor repairs than make finished articles. Then there are the many odd jobs most of us have to do in these days, such as boot-repairing, painting and decorating, looking after the bicycle or the sewing machine, putting in fuses and making additions to electrical installation. There is a great deal to be said for the inclusion of more of these towards the end of the course. If properly handled, each has its educational as well as its utilitarian value.

Finally, there is the problem of vocational training. Before the end of his school life every child turns his mind towards his future livelihood and feels the need for some preparation for it. This drive is one which should not be ignored, for, as we have seen already, lack of interest is one of the greatest difficulties in the Modern School. Clearly, unless the school happens to be in a district where all the school leavers pass into the same industry, the preparation of each for his chosen job is not possible. But much can be done in the first place to help children to choose their jobs, and then for them to investigate and prepare for their choice as far as the school facilities will allow. Visits by the children to factories and workshops, and visits to the school from workers and employers to discuss and describe their work, can form a basis upon which the child can make his first choice. Once this has been made, say towards the beginning of the last year in school, groups can be formed of boys and girls opting for allied trades such as engineering, retail salesmanship, nursing, and clerical work, and each group can collect more information about the work they have chosen. Such research will bring to light any special skills that seem necessary for success in the jobs selected, and practical as well as classroom work can be directed towards the acquisition of such skills as are possible during the remainder of the last year in school.

When we realise the psychological need for a practical approach and both broaden and deepen the content and methods of the new subjects the child meets in the Modern School, we adopt a policy which can have a profound effect upon the new entrant's attitude towards his work. Later in the course, if we stress the utilitarian and finally the vocational value of this side of his education, we shall retain interest, and therefore effort, when it is most needed. The fundamental importance of practical work in the Modern School is thus apparent.

CHAPTER IV

Art, Music, Drama and Physical Education

EDUCATION has the twofold purpose of developing the child as an individual and as a member of society. Certain aspects of education stress one of these aims more than the other. Art, Music, Drama and Physical Education are contrasted because of this and yet they have sufficient in common to justify their consideration in the same chapter.

ART

The child develops his personality through self-expression and the desire for pictorial expression shows itself very early in most children. " New Art " teaching has shown clearly how this desire can be fostered, and its aims and methods have been lucidly explained by Herbert Read in *Education Through Art* (Faber and Faber, 1945). Unfortunately, he neglects the problem which looms largest in the teaching of older children. The young child commits his ideas to paper with very little criticism of the result. To the adult his work may seem crude and haphazard, but the child is satisfied, and that is all that matters.

As the child grows his powers of criticism develop until he begins to be dissatisfied with his pictures. He knows what he wants to portray, but often he fails to achieve the results that he intends because his technique is not adequate. If the matter rests there his interest will flag, and this mode of expression will be lost to the child. In some way or other, therefore, technique must be introduced as the child requires it, while the desire for pictorial expression is retained. The introduction of technique will, for the most part, be incidental, the method depending for its success largely upon the relationship between teacher and child.

Read speaks of the need for the teacher to stand back and

let the child develop. He stresses that much of the wholesome freshness and originality of the child's work can be lost by the undue intrusion of the teacher. To a great extent this is true, but the teacher cannot remain completely in the background. He must be ready to move forward and guide the child as he is required. At first the child is happy portraying things " out of his head," but gradually he begins to look around him for help. Then it is that the teacher can, in response to the child's requests, begin to help him to " see " things. Art is both " seeing " and " doing," and unless a child can first " see " he cannot " do." But what is seen cannot always be simply portrayed. With care a leaf can be drawn which portrays exactly what a leaf is like, but the problem of drawing a tree needs interpretation. In a tree a child sees trunk, branches, twigs and leaves, but he cannot put all these into his picture of a tree. He must therefore learn to look at the tree as a whole and to express what he now sees. This is another instance of that move from the particular to the general which is so difficult for the Modern School child.

The problem can be handled in at least two ways without obtruding too much upon the main stream of expression. Either the teacher can say, " This is how I do it," or he can say, " Let us see how other people have done it." In the first he is tying the child to his own ideas, but, if he follows the second, he is at once leaving the child a free choice, and introducing him to the wider field of Art. Such an introduction is most valuable, provided examples are carefully chosen, for it means that the child has a purpose in looking at good work. This purpose reflects back upon his own work and thus appreciation and execution progress hand in hand. This constant turning to the masters for help and guidance should later be developed into a more direct interest in appreciation which can be fostered by the provision of ample supplies of good reproductions, coupled, where possible, with visits to art galleries.

Artistic expression has not only its pictorial form, it can also be applied in a great variety of ways, and, for the average citizen, the appreciation of what is artistically good in everyday life is even more important than the appreciation of good pictorial art. It therefore follows that the child should be given every opportunity for dealing in his own way with problems of artistic application. Thus, finishing and decorations in needlework, the detail of woodwork models, or even such simple matters as the lay-out of names and subjects on the covers of exercise books, should all be treated as opportunities for artistic expression. Children should discuss and decide the selection and hanging of pictures for their classroom, and the colour schemes and setting of their plays and tableaux.

It follows from this that Art cannot, and should not, be confined to the art room and the art period. To a special degree it is the business of the art teacher, but it is also everybody's business. At all times the importance of striving for perfection and the possibility of individual expression must be appreciated. In this way Art ceases to be specialised. Standards grow which are all-pervading and lead to an attitude which looks for fitness and beauty in everything. If the school sets the example in this, the citizens of the future will demand higher artistic standards and the material things of the world of the future may be less ugly than those that have been tolerated in the past.

MUSIC

Music in school is usually a social rather than an individual activity. It is also one of the activities which the child can carry on after he has left school, if his interest and pleasure in it has been sufficiently aroused during his school days. Thus it is of great inportance in the " education for leisure " we hear so much of nowadays. It follows that the main aim for the music teacher is to see that the children enjoy the subject. This implies choosing the material with care and discretion, and making whatever theory is taught subsidiary to performance. A great deal will depend upon the time that can be spent upon music and upon the capabilities and personal inclinations of the teacher ; but it is clear that over-emphasis on sight reading can do much to spoil enjoyment. The enjoyment, too, must be primarily performers' enjoyment. Too often music is treated as an adjunct to such public functions as prize-givings and the effect upon the audience is the criterion. Such a criterion has its place, for the performer likes to feel that his efforts are appreciated; but a love of music will not be fostered unless enjoyment by the performer is stressed as the main aim.

Appreciation, in the sense of enjoyment from listening, is of great importance, too, but it must develop naturally from performance. It can be introduced by a few remarks about the works that are being sung, and gradually the children can be encouraged to wish to listen to music. Since the child will know most about vocal music it is as well to begin with this. Gramophone records can be obtained of some of the songs the children sing and they can study how these are sung in order to improve their own performances. Later, more ambitious vocal recordings can be played, but the move to orchestral work should be gradual and slow. It will help much if the teacher is a skilled instrumentalist, for then the children can both see and hear. Later, it may be possible to take them to concerts. Those special concerts arranged in big towns for children are most valuable. The aim once more is enjoyment, and knowledge is of value only in so far as it helps towards this end. If the music is handled with these aims in view, there is no reason why the great majority of children leaving the Modern School should not take with them a love of both performing and listening which will be a great asset to them in their later life. It is one of the greatest gifts which the school can offer to the child.

DRAMA

There are all too few chances in school for children to express themselves verbally. In the Modern School children on the whole do not find it easy to express themselves in writing; thus every activity is worth including which will give opportunities for speech. Drama should be used in all its forms, from the simple extempore dramatisation of incidents such as the children will have been used to in their Junior Schools, to more elaborate productions for public exhibition. Clearly the aim here again is enjoyment, for we hope that the child will leave school with a desire to carry on with dramatic work in his leisure time.

In addition to this, drama is one of the most potent forces for integration in school work. Through the production of a play or a musical operetta almost every school subject can be brought together to form a purposeful project. Scenery, staging, dresses, properties, song, dance and speech all play their part in a community effort which can have far-reaching effects upon the atmosphere and tone of the school. Moreover, drama in its various forms can bring out some children who would otherwise remain in the background throughout their school lives. Since it can have so many ramifications, children skilled in many ways can shine, and, with careful selection, it is possible for every child to find himself doing something in which he excels.

Often teachers are discouraged from tackling big dramatic projects because of the mass of organising which they entail, but much of this can be passed on to the children. They should be called upon to take responsibility and to solve their own problems, the teacher acting as co-ordinator and adviser. One of the great difficulties with young people when they leave school is their unwillingness or inability to take responsibility; we should therefore do all we can to provide opportunities for this in school. It must be real responsibility, not the shadow of it with the teacher prodding from behind. If the tone of the group is good there will be plenty of social pressure to make responsible children keep up to the mark. If Drama is skilfully handled it can be a most valuable focus of all-round purposeful work, and can play a vital part in the social education of each child.

PHYSICAL EDUCATION

It may seem strange to deal with Physical Education in the same chapter with Art, Music and Drama, and yet it is another form of individual and social expression. Usually its prime function of physical development overshadows all others; but this is so obvious, and so well dealt with in so many books, that we can afford to take it for granted and to stress one or two of its other functions.

Its importance as a means of social education, with all the " give and take " that this implies, has long been recognised, but its value as a means of individual expression has not been given sufficient attention. For example, the many branches of modern physical education all aim at control and poise, and there is evidence to suggest that improvements in physical co-ordination can lead to similar improvements on the mental plane. These can be seen in the classroom as improved attitudes to work. Again, the opportunities which games give for co-operation and leadership are evident, but more openings could be found for responsibility which, we have seen above, is so much needed today. Children should realise that the privileges of leadership of teams and selection for representative matches carry with them responsibilities which must be shouldered.

The informative side of Physical Education needs much greater emphasis than it has had in the past. No child should leave school until he has an adequate knowledge of the workings of his own body and how it should be cared for. The value of information for its own sake is relative, but none can deny the importance of such knowledge as this. In the next chapter we shall question the paramount importance of an extensive knowledge of historical and geographical facts. But facts which open the child's mind to an understanding of his body, and thus to health and a sound attitude towards himself, fall into quite a different category. No child should leave school without them. Throughout, for simplicity's sake, we have spoken of the pupil as " him " but here it should be specially stressed that the girl is under consideration as well as the boy.

CHAPTER V

The Social Studies

We have now reached the "information" subjects, by which we mean those subjects which are not studied for the acquisition of skills, such as reading and arithmetic, or of taste and enjoyment, such as music and art, or of physical development, but for the information they contain. In the present school curricula these are represented by Geography, History and Civics, and the various branches of Science. For convenience we shall divide these into the Social Studies (i.e., History, Geography and Civics, all studies of man and his works) and Science; and we shall treat these groups separately.

SOCIAL STUDIES AND INFORMATION

As early as 1917, when studying test results, Burt found an affinity between these Social Studies, and he looked upon them as the higher and more "integrative" school subjects, recognising that they called for a considerable skill in reasoning and discrimination if they were to be adequately mastered. Looking at the large majority of schemes of work and studying the text books usually found in schools, we find that they demand or present an imposing array of facts arranged in a comprehensive whole. In other words, they present to the child a careful summary of the information available in the subject concerned, and we cannot but feel that any child who mastered them would be a well-informed adult.

Do we find, in fact, that, after a generation or two of this, the population is well informed? Do we find that people as a whole wish to be well informed? We have to be careful in answering this, for we must think of the sort of people we possibly do not meet in our everyday life. But if we have knocked about a little, been in the Forces perhaps, or even the Home Guard or Civil Defence, and have thus met on an equal footing the adults who have passed through our old Elementary Schools, it is difficult not to agree that the level of simple general information is not high. Certainly it is not so high as the schemes of work and the textbooks would have led us to expect. * Why is this? What have we been trying to do?

Let us remember that a set of facts mean nothing to a child unless he can fully grasp and understand the concepts that lie behind them. This has clearly been recognised for a long time, for we have laid great emphasis upon the importance of using pictures, actual examples, films, broadcasts and so on, to enliven our work and enable children to build up the concepts more easily. To some extent we have succeeded, and children today have a far better chance of understanding the things they are learning about than previously. The emphasis, however, is still upon knowledge, which in itself is not a bad thing, but is there another way of looking at the problem?

SOCIAL STUDIES AND ACTIVITY

Let us think for a moment of the work of the American educationist Dewey, which has had such a great effect upon the trend of education in his own country. He placed great emphasis upon the place of *experience* in education, and his followers developed from his teaching the idea of the " Activity School " in which subjects and formal instruction give way to widespread and varied activity, both collective and individual. Time-tables went by the board and with them class-teaching, and each child engaged in whatever work or play he set his heart on. The idea behind this was that the learning of such skills and reading and calculating came along naturally as the child felt the need for them. With specially gifted children, a mass of varied equipment and a high proportion of teachers to children, this may be possible.

The best description of a school of this sort in operation, which gives very full details of every phase of the work, can be found in *Curriculum Records of the Children's School*, by members of the Staff (Bureau of Publications, National College of Education, Illinois, 1940). Personally, I feel that

* See *History, Heritage and Environment* by H. B. McNichol (Faber, 1946)

with schools as they are today, and with the children who come to the Modern School, more framework is needed in the day's work, the children need more guidance and support, and more economy of time and effort is needed than an activity school can give. Yet there is a great deal to be said for activity and interest, and much that can be learnt from the methods of the " Activity School." Such schools do not set out to teach facts, they aim at arousing interest and feel that the facts will follow.

We have already seen that our teaching has improved in recent years because it has become more real. Why not keep this reality but divorce it from the aim of turning out a well-informed citizen? Make the aim that of allowing the child's interest and awareness to expand and then see whether the facts will follow. The facts may not be so well marshalled or as comprehensive as we intended them to be in the past, but, to the child, were they ever really that? Did he attend every day of the year and pay steady attention at each lesson? Let " 1066 and All That," and books of " Schoolboy Howlers," be our warning! However systematic our facts and however complete our scheme, did not even the best student leave us with a few well-remembered patches and a great many arid expanses in between? Did we ever ourselves gain a well-grounded knowledge of History and Geography until we either had to get them up for examination, or to teach them? Thus what do we lose if we throw away our carefully planned schemes of work, and our textbooks, too, for that matter, except as reference books, and make our main aim awareness and interest through activity?

The word " awareness " is used here advisedly, for in Brighton a year or two back I carried out an experiment to investigate the differences between Senior School and Grammar School boys, and it came out most clearly from test results that one of the main differences was that the Senior School boys were less " aware " than those who had been selected for the Grammar School. They were also less intelligent, but it was not a question of ability to reason or remember, but simply a marked inability to see things as they were, to grasp and comprehend the simple things around them. Does it not thus again seem that it is better to help these children to develop their awareness rather than set ourselves to plan ways or means of presenting to them facts which they will, quite likely, never make their own, and thus forget all too quickly?

The idea presented here is far from new and in many schools fine work is being done along these lines; but there are still so many of our colleagues who have not yet seen the reason for a change of this sort that it must be argued at some length.

THE NEED FOR PURPOSE

Let us see now how the idea can be, and is being, put into practice, and how it can be fitted into the other activities of the school curriculum.

We are to exchange the scheme of work for the project, and, as will be shown later when time-tables are discussed, we are allowing a minimum of some six or eight periods a week for this activity. The projects can be long or short and their subjects will vary considerably with the environment of the school and the inclination of the staff. " What is one man's meat is another man's poison," is truer than ever when we think of teaching, so that it would be hopeless to try to plan anything in detail, but general principles, examples and references to published work may help to stimulate ideas and suggest lines for action.

The first and fundamental principle is that there must be purpose, and this purpose must be that of the children. It will often arise from the teacher who will have many higher purposes behind those that became apparent to the children, but the ostensible purpose of the work must be accepted by the children as their own. In other words, the teacher may think, " This will help their reading or their calculating; it will enable them to know their home town better or to understand the point of view of other peoples in the world; it will help them to develop the habit of finding out facts for themselves or critically to examine facts passed on to them." The children, on the other hand, must say, " This is something worth while doing, something I want to do."

Let us take our first hint from that actuality and reality which, we saw above, have improved our teaching of subjects in recent years. There is tremendous scope around every school, whether in town or country, for bringing children into contact with their environment. Ask the children in your class a few questions about their own neighbourhoods and you will be astonished, if you are not so already, how little they know about them. There is thus plenty of scope here and the school can gain access to many places that the individual children cannot, so that much more can be done in groups than any individual child can hope to do himself. Get the children out of the schools and into the streets and the country-side. What will they do when they get there? We are all too familiar with the school visit which was inevitably followed by the demand for an account of what had been seen. How can this be varied and enlivened?

A SIMPLE SCHOOL VISIT

First there must be planning beforehand on the part of the children. They should have a hand in making the arrangements. Parents are helpful in making the necessary contacts, letters have to be written and possibly costs and transport worked out, and the children should play a part in this. Then there is the preparation for the visit. What should the children know about the place before they visit it? Suppose it is a gas or electricity works or a factory to which older children in the school have already been. Let one or two of them come to the class for an hour and talk to the children about it, or answer questions, so that the new group begins to find out what it is likely to see when they go, and decide what they want to look for. They can make notes of things they would specially like to see so that they do not miss them on the tour, or of questions they will ask when they get there. These can be either collected for the group as a whole, or, as the children become more used to the work, produced individually. The children are now primed, and when the day arrives they will get much more out of the visit than they would have done without preparation.

After the visit, at which a few children who have been before can act as assistant guides if it seems advisable, a discussion can take place during which recollections can be exchanged and questions answered. From this it may appear that interest has been aroused in certain matters which are worth following up, and this can lead to further visits or studies. Thus a project is born. It could also spring from other sources, of course, but, whatever its origin, how can it be developed and sustained ? This is dealt with in the next chapter.

CHAPTER VI.

THE DEVELOPMENT OF PROJECTS

The well-informed citizen is not the man who knows all there is to know, but rather he who is sufficiently interested in current happenings to absorb information about them as they arise, and who knows how to find any additional information he requires. This is another way of saying that education goes on throughout life, a phrase which is close to the lips of most educators today. To produce such citizens schools must, in the Social Studies, place activity and interest before information, and this is the attitude developed by the project approach.

If teachers who use the project method needed a motto it might well be, " Look after interest and drive, and let the facts look after themselves." We have already seen that one of the problems of the Secondary Modern School is that the children show so little interest in their work, but that their interest can be easily aroused by visits to places of special interest in their environment. It is moreover true that, at first, their interest in any one thing tends to wane quickly. It follows therefore that care must be taken in choosing the first visits and no project should be spread over too long a period. A lesson or two given to preparation for the visit and a similar period for the drawing of conclusions should cover the project, and all this can be concentrated in a week's work. To drag it out to a greater length or even to spread it over too long a period can easily spell failure in these early and vital days.

A SIMPLE PROJECT

It is clear from what has now been said that a simple project consists of three parts ; preparation for experience, the experience itself, and the consideration and recording of the experience. The first must be approached as a corporate effort on the part of both teacher and children. At first the teacher will take a considerable part in guiding and stimulating effort but, as time goes on, he will be able to drop more and more into the background, while ensuring that the children have what they need to prepare for the next step.

Suppose the children are to visit the local gas works. A general discussion will quickly bring out the fact that the children know quite a lot about the gas works already. They will know where the works are and roughly what is done there. They can recognise a gas-holder, and will have seen coal coming to the works and coke going away. As the discussion develops it will be clear that there are gaps in their information, so the children can help to make one list of the things they would like to know before they make the visit, and another list of the things they would like to see and to find out when they get there. The next period can be given to filling up some of these gaps. There are many ways of doing this. The most obvious sources of information are books and the teacher, but it may be possible to obtain information at first hand. It was suggested earlier that one way is to fill in the gaps by consulting children in other classes who have visited the place on previous occasions. They can be brought in for a period and questioned by the new class. Or there may be a child in the class whose father is employed at the gas works, who can be given the task of obtaining information from his father and reporting back. A more real source can be tapped if the child's father, or somebody connected with the works, can come to the class to answer the questions himself. Notice that the visitor is not asked to give a lecture. A lecture is useful, but then the children are passive ; if they get the information they want by questioning it is likely to be of more value to them, even if, to the adult mind, it seems to be less comprehensive.

If all these methods fail a series of pictures can be shown and the class can discuss them, asking the teacher to explain this and that. A film could be used, but possibly still pictures would be better on an occasion like this since they give more opportunity for discussion. If there is time the children could possibly make gas themselves, using clay pipes, or some more elaborate form of apparatus to facilitate study of the by-products.

When the preparation is complete the child is ready for the visit. Not only does he know something about the things he is going to see but he also knows what to look for on the visit. Moreover he is setting out in the right frame of mind to absorb all he can from the visit, which is what really matters. Often visits are disappointing since the noise and bustle of a works and, at times, the inadequacy of the guide, make it difficult for the child to find out all he wants. It helps therefore if each child has with him a copy of the points the class has decided to look for and the questions to which they have decided to seek answers.

After a visit a period can be spent in discussing the list each child has taken with him. In this way gaps can be filled up and experiences shared. Possibly new questions will be raised which can be investigated briefly. Finally some record of the visit should be made. We all know the sigh that comes from a class when they are asked to " Write an account of the visit." The children are filled with ideas but it is no easy matter to reduce this mass to a simple and coherent account. One of the simplest ways to solve this problem is to let the class decide what topics the account can be divided into, and then let small groups get together to compose a brief note on each. These notes are then written up and the whole bound in a folder as a class record. The folder will have to have a cover and, possibly, illustrations, so that the artists in the class will have full scope. A great deal of time could be spent on this stage of the work but it is wise at first to limit it, so that interest does not wane.

All experienced teachers know that however good a method or technique may be it loses its value if it is used too often. It is therefore important that projects and the way in which they are dealt with should be as varied as possible. Here are one or two suggestions :

(1) " Let us find out what our town was like in grandfather's

time." The children can collect the information at home and then pool it in school. It may be possible to collect a small exhibition of photographs and things that were in use in grandfather's day.

(2) " What is it like to be a policeman ? " Bring a policeman into this if it is possible.

(3) " How do the locks on the canal work ? "

(4) " How do they put a goods train together ? "

(5) " What happens to the rubbish collected from our dustbins ? "

All these can be dealt with more simply than the visit to the gas works, but along similar lines. It is easy to add to this list in both number and variety of subjects. The children can, and should, make most of the suggestions for further work, the teacher guiding them to choose possible and profitable topics.

PROJECTS IN SERIES

If the children have been used to project work in the Primary School progress to more ambitious projects can be more rapid, but it is better to go too slowly than too quickly since we must not exceed the children's interest span. As a transition, projects can be linked in series, though the items in the series need not necessarily follow directly upon each other. Thus, for town children, visits to a farm not too far distant on four or five occasions during the year can do much to enable them to appreciate the importance of country life and its annual round. The value of such visits can be enhanced if the children from the village school act as guides, the town school children returning the compliment when the village children visit the town. In an article in *The Times Educational Supplement*, (28th Oct., 1944), exchanges of this sort which lasted several days were described, but visits lasting only an hour or two can be most valuable. In this way town and village children get to know one another better and each learns not only about the new environment, but also more of his own environment by acting as a guide to it.

From a visit to the gas works can develop a series dealing with the local services and, in the same way, from a study of life in grandfather's time can grow a series reaching back and back into history, using old buildings, museum exhibits and old maps and records to illustrate and enliven the work.

MORE COMPREHENSIVE PROJECTS

The final stage is to set about a larger problem demanding a more thorough investigation. Here are a few of the topics which suggest themselves :

(1) " What are we doing to make the roads safer and how can we improve this ? "

(2) " What do we pay rates for ? "

(3) " How could our town be improved ? "

(4) " Who built the churches we see around us and what was it like to live when the work was going on ? "

(5) " What can we find out about our local industries, and why have they grown up here ? "

(6) " What does a Borough Councillor do ? "

In the earlier simple projects, visits play an important part, but in these later and larger schemes, although visits may still play a very important part, more time is spent in seeking information from books, for the children are older and thus more able to cope with these sources of information. It is easy to see also how technique can develop. The discussion can become the more formal debate ; children can stage Council meetings, elections and trials by jury : they can enact pageants of local history, and set up exhibitions to illustrate life and work in other countries ; they can form committees to ensure greater safety for those coming to school on bicycles, run sports days and savings drives. The great value that can be derived from the production of musical and dramatic performances has already been stressed.

SOME PROJECT PROBLEMS

To be effective all projects must have an aim which appeals to the children, and must show some tangible results. In the earlier and simpler projects this aim is within the project itself, consisting of the visit round which many of the projects are centred. But it is often a help to interest if there is the further aim that the work is worth doing not only for itself but also for its results. Thus a secondary aim in a visit can be to produce a record for a class diary, and, at times, this secondary aim can, with a useful stimulation of interest, assume predominance in the eyes of the children.

For example, it helps to work up the material into such a form that it can be shown to others as an exhibition. In London, where the outward movement of population had, before the war, emptied some of the school buildings, an experiment was on foot to use certain empty schools as exhibition centres for their localities, and it was hoped that many of the exhibitions in them would be produced and run by the schools themselves. In a similar way I found that great zest was added to local study when the children were asked to prepare an exhibition about Camberwell to go to the other Camberwells in various parts of the Empire, in exchange for similar studies from them. But exhibitions need not all be as ambitious as this. The preparation of work for an open day, or merely the setting up of a show for other classes to see, gives point to the work. Or, following up a suggestion made in the previous chapter, the guiding of visiting children is a secondary purpose that may loom large to the children.

GRAPHS AND SYMBOLS

This idea of a secondary motive which exists in the result of the study brings us to a consideration of the way in which results can be recorded. There will be some children, especially in the " A " classes, who can handle written work in a competent fashion, but there will be many who can better express themselves in other ways. Illustration of all kinds, including the laying out of title pages and the decorating of covers, gives ample scope for the artistic. Indications of other possibilities come from the great development in recent years of the use of diagrams, graphs and symbols for the stating of facts.

Graphs themselves have their uses, but little men, houses, factory chimneys and the like, showing facts either by their number or by their size, have taken more and more space on posters and in papers in recent years. It would be fair to say that no child should leave school until he has learnt to interpret such matter easily and accurately, as a part of his education. And what better way is there to do this than through its practical use?

Maps and diagrams also are both useful and educational. The drawing of maps is a long and tedious process but the use of a base map upon which information can be shown is simple, quick and effective. Base maps can be duplicated and local areas may in some cases be available on " Mapograph " rollers or similar devices. For more detailed maps of the home district it used to be possible to purchase quite cheaply from the Ordnance Survey quantities of any area on the six-inch scale at reasonable prices, and these facilities may soon return. Models of all sorts are fascinating to children and can be simply constructed in a variety of ways. Photography too should play its part. Every possible method of recording facts should be tried out, for in this way the varied abilities of the class can be used and the interest maintained.

CLASS ORGANISATION

This brings up the problem of class organisation. The earlier projects will clearly be worked by the group as a whole, since this is the simpler method with novices, but soon it will be possible for small groups to be formed for simple and specific purposes. A mixture of class and group work will until experience has been gained form the basis of much of the early projects. Later, when the children are more skilled in both collecting information and presenting it, individual work is the ideal. But it is essential, if the teacher wishes to remain sane, that individual work should not be embarked upon too soon.

Individual work calls for a great deal of initiative on the part of the children, for it is clear that children must be able to carry on with a minimum of personal supervision. There is no reason why individual children should not be given special work to do from time to time from the very beginning, but to have a class all making individual contributions to a communal effort, or each engaged upon his own project, calls for a high degree of individual responsibility and skill. On the other hand the class which can carry out projects in this way is surely showing the value of its early training, and getting the most it can from the work.

It will clearly be seen from the examples and suggestions already given that most of these projects can be labelled History, Geography or Civics. Why then should we bother to cut adrift from the subject arrangement of our time tables? Why not merely introduce the project element into each course using the periods allotted to each subject. There are two arguments against this. In the first place it would be unwise to ask children to interest themselves in two or three projects simultaneously for their interests would thus be divided and muddled; and in the second place this would mean that even a simple project would be spread over a number of weeks. It thus seems better to pool the time that can be allowed to these subjects, stealing a little additional from the English periods since so much of the work will involve discussion and a search for information, and, to perhaps a lesser degree, the writing up of results, and to devote all this to one project at a time. Clearly the teacher must guide the choice of studies so that useful fields are covered in a truly educational manner. In this way children will still have the opportunity of developing that historical sense, that conception of the interdependence of the world today and that feeling of civic responsibility which are some of the main aims of History, Geography and Civics teaching.

There is no reason however why the project should be closely bound to so many periods a week, for many opportunities will occur for its tentacles to spread into other parts of the time-table. This spread can be sporadic, the acceptance or rejection of the possibilities offered being dependent upon the individual teacher's wishes and the way things work out. Art, handiwork, science, arithmetic, practically every school subject can be brought into the orbit of the project if necessary, and, since we have seen that the basis of project work is the drive that comes from purpose, this will be to the benefit of the subject invaded.

SOURCES OF REFERENCE

One of the practical difficulties of project work, which is also from the educational point of view one of its advantages, is the need for an ample provision of textbooks, maps, reference books, pamphlets, tables of statistics, and the like from which children can collect information. In the earlier stages this is less important, for much can be done with the pooled knowledge of the class and such direct observation as they can make themselves, but the need for other sources of information soon grows. To a certain extent this demand can be met since there will be a dropping off in the need for sets of textbooks, so a greater variety can be purchased, Moreover, children should be encouraged to forage for themselves in libraries and elsewhere. However, project work will be helped enormously if authorities realise that, in the initial stages especially, adequate funds should be available for the purchase of a wide variety of text and reference books so that the children's efforts are not frustrated.

There is a very wide field from which information can be drawn that is outside the usual classroom material. Guide-books, travel brochures and booklets of special topics such as those on country affairs produced by the Young Farmers' Clubs are some of the many sources. It is not always easy to see just how such information can be used in class, for it often has a value apart from its use as a reference.

One of the beauties of projects is that they can be so easily adapted, not only to the children and the locality but also to the teacher's special interests and knowledge. Thus I have always been interested in the local study side of project work and a summary of a survey of the Borough of Camberwell carried out just before the war may be useful as an example of an extensive project. It was started as an experiment to see what local work could be done in such an unpromising area as a London borough, and the enthusiasm and zest with which the children took up the work and carried it through convinced me once and for all of the merits of the project method.

A LOCAL STUDY PROJECT

It consisted of maps, diagrams, models and collections of one sort and another, recording information under the following headings :

(1) The Position of Camberwell. Its relation to London, to the London Basin and to other London Boroughs. Borough Boundaries old and new, and the relation of the old boundaries to the hills and valleys of the district.

(2) The Streams, Hills and Valleys of Camberwell and their relation to the wider features of the London Basin. The way in which these have influenced the development of roads, settlement, old farming, population distribution and types of houses.

(3) The Rocks which lie under Camberwell, and life on the earth when they were laid down. The effect of these rocks on old water supply, settlement, soils and farming, road making and the making of bricks and tiles.

(4) The Climate of Camberwell, compared with other places in similar latitudes.

(5) The Farming which was carried on in Camberwell in 1745, 1760-5, and 1837-42.

(6) The Industries of Camberwell in 1870 and today. The relative importance of different manufactures. Exhibits by Camberwell manufacturers of the goods they make.

(7) The Trade of Camberwell ; main shopping centres.

(8) Travel in Camberwell. Ancient roads and trackways.

Roads in the Eighteenth Century. Scenes on the old roads. Transport facilities today and the relative accessibility of various parts of the Borough. The increase of traffic at Camberwell Green and a comparison between traffic there and in other parts of the Borough. The Grand Surrey Canal, its history and past and present importance.

(9) The People of Camberwell. The growth of population, and present population compared with other boroughs in London and other towns in England and the Empire. The growth of population in the parts of the Borough since 1745. The main occupations of the people of Camberwell and changes which are taking place in these occupations. The movement of people to and from Camberwell for their work. Famous people who have lived in Camberwell.

(10) Where people have settled in Camberwell. The earliest people. The Doomsday Manors, and Manors of the Middle Ages. The gradual growth of Camberwell since 1610 illustrated by old maps. The different types of neighbourhood in Camberwell today. Camberwell parks and open spaces.

(11) How the everyday wants of Camberwell are supplied. The work of the Borough Council, the London County Council and Parliament in providing the necessary services in Camberwell. The water, gas, electricity, milk and coal supply The Police. The Post Office and the Telephone service.

OTHER STARTING POINTS

Two other cores for projects are worth mentioning. The School Journey is not merely an adjunct to the school course, but a real centre round which much valuable work and experience can be concentrated. Then there is the Ship Adoption Society which provides for its members such a useful springboard for study. It may be helpful also to mention one or two books in which descriptions of projects can be found.

Village Survey-making. An Oxfordshire Experiment. H.M. Stationery Office, 1929.

Local Studies. Geographical Association, 1939.

Education for Citizenship in Elementary Schools. Association for Education in Citizenship, 1939.

"*School Visits School*" Article in *The Times Educational Supplement* by S. V. Perfect, Headmaster of Hatters Lane S.B. School, High Wycombe, 28th October, 1944.

CHAPTER VII

SCIENCE AND THE SCIENTIFIC ATTITUDE

SCIENCE, like the Social studies is an " information " subject, but the study of Science should lead not only to factual knowledge but also to that attitude of mind which distinguishes the thought of modern times from that of the Middle Ages. This scientific attitude is characterised by the replacement of dogma by reason, prejudice by balanced judgment and tacit acceptance by intelligent investigation.

If these traits were typical of the thought of the masses we should not expect to find people so influenced by slogans and propaganda, ruled by prejudices and attracted to such futilities as astrology, as they appear to be. Yet a willingness to weigh and balance evidence, a striving to understand a situation and an ability to form a sound judgment are needed by all citizens of a democracy, if such a democracy is to be living and real. It is therefore important that the Secondary Modern School, in which the bulk of future electors will receive their education, should strive to develop this questioning spirit in its children. That is why it is worth while to spend some time considering the part which can be played by the scientific attitude in school work as a whole before we discuss the teaching of Science.

DEMOCRACY AND THE SCIENTIFIC ATTITUDE

We have heard much in recent years of the authoritarian form of state in which facts and principles laid down by the rulers must be accepted without question by all citizens. This has been condemned by all democratic thinking people, yet the same authoritarian attitude in our schools has led to a far smaller outcry. Those who have protested have, as must be expected, dispensed with authority wholesale ; Homer Lane and A. S. Neill can be numbered among them. They have, however, thrust too great a responsibility upon the immature child and, although there is much that can be learned from their experiments, it is generally recognised that their methods are too extreme to be followed by the generality. How, then, can a balance between authority and licence be attained ? It is this middle way which is always so difficult to discover. It can be called the way of " liberty " and contrasted to " authority " on the one hand and " licence " on the other ; it is associated with " self-control " as opposed to " imposed control " and " anarchy."

Both liberty and self-control can be regarded as being, in part, attitudes of mind. That is, although they are themselves influenced by happenings, they can also exert their influence upon events, thus producing circumstances favouring their own continuance. This seems to show that in discussing attitudes we are dealing with something fundamental and not significant to a part of the curriculum alone. Such is the case, and we must therefore take a broad basis for our further consideration of the problem, which is none other than, " How can the school best develop that attitude of mind in its pupils which will make them good citizens of a democracy in a scientific age ? "

Attitudes are infectious so that much depends upon the atmosphere of the school, and this in turn depends upon those who teach in it. Teachers must be prepared to approach problems with an open mind, to search for and assess all relative evidence and then to attempt a considered solution based upon this. Such a training in critical method may come from many different subjects and fields of study. Its effect upon the individual is to develop that humility which comes from a realisation of the smallness of one's knowledge, in direct contrast to the cock-sureness which accompanies superficial acquaintance.

To guide other seekers, the teacher must himself be a seeker and not a know-all. The key-note must be : " Let us try to find out," rather than : " I will tell you." It is only the teacher who is unwilling to accept without question the findings of others who can himself engender in his pupils the questioning attitude of the good democrat. The importance of this attitude can be judged from the cynical principles by which the Nazis developed their unfortunately successful propaganda both at home and abroad. " If you say a thing often enough and with sufficient loudness, everybody will believe it." " Men do not think, they feel ; therefore it is enough to appeal to the emotions and forget the intellect." Less cynically but with just as much success, advertisers build up the reputations of their wares. Democracy cannot thrive in such a world, and therefore the school must enable the children to appreciate something different.

THE TEACHING OF SCIENCE

The development of this scientific attitude is part and parcel of the entire curriculum, but it is only able to display itself as far as matter and technique make its development possible. In the tool subjects, such as Reading and Arithmetic, there are few opportunities, compared with the obvious chances project work offers for just this sort of thing. Here, then, is yet another argument for the project approach. How does it apply to its own subject matter, Science ? If we aimed at providing in the Secondary Modern School an organised groundwork in Science so that our children could pass to higher study in the subject our way could be clearer, but this is the function of other types of Secondary School, for our children have neither the ability, the inclination nor the time for this.

Shall we water down the organised course ? This means teaching the children what we think they ought to know, which is neither advisable nor necessary. Much advanced scientific research is fundamentally empirical. Sir Oliver Lodge used to tell his young assistants when they started on a new problem to forget all they knew about it, neglect the literature and work from first principles ; Edison tried everything he could think of, including Limburger cheese, before he found a filament for his first electric lamp ; Fleming accidentally discovered penicillin. All these men, in addition to being able to draw upon a great depth of scientific knowledge, were ready to " see what would happen " and to seize chance observations. In the far simpler matters with which we deal in the Secondary Modern School a similar attitude can be adopted. Much scientific research is done, of necessity, with apparatus devised by the researcher; he cannot turn to a traditional method of carrying out his unique experiments. Thus it is fair to allow children to find their own ways and means of setting up and carrying out simple experiments.

Our Science work should spring from the problems which the children themselves feel the need for answering; it can be sporadic rather than comprehensive; it will largely consist of the " let's see what will happen " sort of experiment set up after their own fashion by the children themselves. Two further points. If the problem is one to which the children already know the answer it is waste of time to do it. Each experiment must be a genuine search for information; yet each must give the children a chance of success and must therefore call neither for too high a level of fundamental knowledge nor for too advanced a technique.

SOME EXAMPLES OF METHOD

Let us take an example. The heating of homes, schools and other buildings is a topic of interest and practical importance to both boys and girls. One of the problems connected with it is the reason for placing the furnace in the basement of the school. If this is discussed in class a number of suggestions will be made. These can be discussed and some of them disposed of at once. Before a solution is accepted the class should decide to make a model so that they can try out the effect of placing the furnace in different positions. The model can be simply set up with flasks, corks, glass-tubing and a bunsen burner and then different layouts can be tried. From the findings of these experiments deductions can lead to the principle of convection.

A word about class discussions seems to be in place here. Discussions can range from the formal debate and the one-sided affair in which the teacher labours by questioning to dig information and opinions from the children, to the free-for-all heated argument which arises when matters which the children feel very keenly are discussed. All three have their place but in cases like that mentioned above the best work can be done in discussions in which the teacher is there as an unobtrusive and unstyled chairman to see fair play, to put a question at times to help things along and to give information if he is asked for it, but in which the main activity is a free give-and-take between the children themselves. The value of such discussions to the children can be judged by the number of children taking part and the degree to which they stimulate each other to thought and provoke each other to speech. Such discussions will only come if the subject is real to the children and the reason for discussion clear. That is, there must be real purpose. The way a discussion runs will soon show whether this is present or not.

It would be wrong if experiments always came out with positive answers. In a country school the children came to the teacher with the old theory that seeds must be planted at certain phases of the moon to ensure good crops. Some boys doubted this, and so it was decided to try it. Long discussions followed on the planning of the experiment which eventually got under way with all sorts of safeguards to ensure the accuracy of the result. No difference was found in the crops, but the theorists were not satisfied and planned even more careful and elaborate experiments which were carried out the following year, again failing to confirm their theory. This was a most valuable piece of scientific work for all concerned; it sprang naturally from the children themselves and was excellent training in both scientific method and attitude.

PURELY INFORMATIONAL WORK

Clearly the ground that can be covered in this way is limited and many of the questions to which children seek the answers are not suitable for experimental treatment. There is thus room for a good deal of purely informational work in Science, the information often being of direct utilitarian value to the children and springing from their own expressed seeking. Much of this can develop naturally from the project carried on in connection with the Social Sciences. Thus a visit to a gas works has its civic side when we consider gas supply as a social service, and its scientific side when we consider the production of the gas itself. Simple experiments can be planned by the children to see what happens when you bake coal, but the finer points of the by-products of the industry call for information rather than for more elaborate experiment.

This is a scientific age and it is apt that the fundamentally questioning attitude of the age should run right through the curriculum of our Secondary Modern School. We have seen how this can be done by freeing the curriculum from its authoritarian inheritance of information, setting the pupils free to quest and seek for themselves as far as their capacities and abilities will allow.

CHAPTER VIII

Problems of Grading and Specialisation

The problems of organisation in the Secondary Modern School are no less formidable than those of curriculum, and they also need thinking out from fundamentals.

Let us take a group of youngsters just up from their various Primary Schools. Either we have received with them their Primary School Record Cards, and thus know a great deal about their attainment and abilities, or we can put them through a series of tests, such as those suggested in an earlier chapter, to assess them. Having obtained this information the next problem is grading.

WHY DO WE GRADE?

Let us start at the beginning and ask ourselves why we grade children. The answer is that children's abilities vary and it is therefore more convenient to have children of more or less equal ability in each class. That sounds very simple until we ask, " What type of ability do you grade by ? " Sometimes children are graded according to Intelligence; but this takes no account of attainment, which may vary considerably within each group. Too often grading is carried out by some simple tests in which Arithmetic plays far too important a part. But whatever branch of attainment is used as the basis for grading, it will be upset very soon by the effect of the new school upon each child. Some will be stimulated by a new approach and go ahead while others find new difficulties and fall back. Thus any grading needs frequent revision if it is to be worth while.

ADVANTAGES AND DISADVANTAGES OF GRADING

Grading has its disadvantages, too. It necessitates the labelling of certain children " B " or " C," that is, as inferiors to the general run, and this sense of inferiority is already, as we have seen earlier, one of the greatest handicaps which children in these schools have to overcome. We cannot get over the difficulty by calling " B " and " C " streams by another name ; the children soon find out. In one school, which had in days gone by been inspected by Matthew Arnold as H.M.I., the backward class was called the " Arnold Class " (I never discovered why), but even this did not fool the children ; the stigma was still there. If we decide not to grade it must be a true decision. Camouflaged grading will deceive nobody.

How far is grading by attainment an advantage? It certainly helps in the tool subjects of reading and arithmetic, but it matters much less in art, which is an individual subject, and music and physical education, which are largely group activities. Handicraft is largely individual, although it helps to have children of a fairly even grading ; but how often do we notice the duffer at sums who can do beautiful work in handicraft, thus showing again that grading which suits one subject need not necessarily suit another? If, as has been suggested in some detail in geography, history, civics and science, the stress is placed upon activity rather than information, the possibility of suiting the work to the individual comes right to the fore and the need for grading takes a back seat. Thus it is the tool subjects that seem to benefit most from grading.

GRADING AND THE TOOL SUBJECTS

In arithmetic, upon the mechanical side, the problem is not so much that the children have not covered the ground ; they are likely to have been over the rules time and time again, but they will have gaps in their information. These gaps will vary from child to child and can best be tackled by individual methods. The use of individual methods is, at the moment, seriously hampered by lack of suitable textbooks, so that some sort of grading may be the only compromise. But need the grading for arithmetic be spread over into other subjects? In many schools the time-table is so arranged that children are re-graded throughout the school for this subject. Here is one solution for arithmetic.

Reading is the key to English, so what about reading? But reading is the approach to many other subjects, too, for reading skill is fundamentally important, and here, I feel, is a real basis for grading. But it need only affect those children, and they will be the minority, who have not reached a moderate standard. All those who can read a simple text such as they are likely to encounter in looking up information for themselves, or in reading for pleasure, can go ahead and need not be graded in this way.

We are therefore left in the First Year of a Secondary Modern School with a group of, say, one third of the entrants who need grouping together because of their reading disabilities, while the remaining two-thirds, although they may be re-classified for arithmetic, can be divided into cross-sections according to any other standards for the bulk of their work.

The group which is placed together for reading should be as small as circumstances will allow, and they should know exactly why they are there. I have yet to come across the Senior School boy who does not realise the necessity for acquiring the skill and who does not jump at the chance of the individual help that such cases require. The whole reading problem is less acute with girls. At the end of the first year the teacher will know enough about each of the children of this group to say whether his individual problems are capable of solution. By this time the residue of non-readers will be constitutional illiterates and these should be passed to such classes as cater for children needing special treatment.

By resolute attack the reading problem should be solved by the end of the first year and the basis for grading should thus disappear. From then on classes should be communities rather than grades and thus one of the greatest emotional obstacles be removed from the paths of the less intelligent children. Each child in these communities should possess sufficent skill in the tool subjects so that he can use these tools in projects based upon individual activity and so develop his mastery of the tools further by their application.

DISADVANTAGES OF SPECIALISATION

The N.U.T. Report of 1939 upon the training of teachers states (p. 56) : " Many of our witnesses held the view that too great a degree of specialisation in the Senior School is not advantageous. . . . It may lead to the subjects taught taking precedence over what should be the teacher's real purpose—the complete development of the child." That is a clear statement of one disadvantage of specialisation, but there are others which spring from the characteristics of the child who comes to the Secondary Modern School. Teachers who have had any experience of these children cannot help remarking the adverse effect that lack of continuity and stability of schooling has upon them. This has been especially marked during the war years when evacuation and the drift back, and the necessity for constant staff changes, has broken the stream of their education in many ways. When things are going smoothly they progress ; they need stability. To this we must add the fact that, to a greater or lesser degree, each child is a problem case needing individual understanding and treatment. With classes of forty or fifty what chance is there of such treatment ? Even the thirties we look for, but which seem so far off, will still leave the problem of individual handling a very great one for the teacher to face. Specialisation adds to this difficulty, for it adds to the number of children each teacher has to know and to the number of teachers to whom each child has to adapt himself. Thus the problem seems to rest upon a decision between the subject and the child, change and stability, the individual and the group.

ADVANTAGES OF SPECIALISATION

But specialisation has its advantages, too. To know your subject and to be an enthusiast for it is a stimulant to both teacher and children. It also means that the teacher can survey the possibilities of his subject and select those parts and aspects of it that are most suitable to the group of children with whom he is dealing. Notice that these are reasons for specialisation, but that they stress the subject rather than the child. In certain subjects, either because they tend to be more emotional or because they deal with groups rather than individuals, the plea for specialisation appears to be most pressing. Thus to teach Art special ability and interest on the part of the teacher is most desirable, while in Physical Education the youth of the teacher and the fact that it is essentially a group activity, together with the dangers which attend inexpert handling, suggest specialisation. Music falls into both these categories, for it needs special ability on the part of the teacher, and is also a group activity. Handicraft and Domestic Science again call for specialised training and this implies specialisation, but one cannot help wishing that the former, since it is so sound an approach to other things for the majority of Modern School children, could be more closely wedded to the course as a whole instead of being shut off in its water-tight compartment, to the disadvantage both of itself and the whole curriculum. The tool subjects of Arithmetic and English are better worked in with the Social Studies to form the core of the curriculum and taken by the class teacher. Re-classification for arithmetic would, of course, cut across this. Science lies on debatable ground, and depends largely upon the abilities of those who form the school staff and the manner in which the subject is handled.

A SOLUTION TO THE PROBLEM

A solution to this problem would thus seem to be that each class teacher should handle the whole of the work of his form except Art, Physical Education, Music, Handicraft or Domestic subjects and probably Science, thus giving a solid core of some half of the time to stable and individual work concentrating upon the development of the child. Finally, yet another point of view on specialisation is expressed by Stead in *The*

Education of a Community (p. 134) : " When teachers themselves realise the true foundations of educational effort, and are themselves integrated personalities infused with the purpose of the good community, then many of the present evils of specialisation will disappear."

This concept of the teacher and his function brings us to the core of the problem of education. It all depends upon the teacher. No scheme of work, no method of presentation, no testing programme can replace the benefit which comes from good teaching. Nor can anybody use schemes, methods or programmes satisfactorily unless he is a good teacher. Good teaching is more than knowing the tricks of the trade, it is something which depends fundamentally upon the personality and philosophical outlook of the teacher. All good teachers realise this and strive to see their work in its widest aspect, seeking the aims and principles underlying instruction, treating the instruction itself as incidental although having its own share of importance both as a means and as an end. However much stress is laid upon this attitude in training courses, it can never be fully appreciated until thoughtful experience and maturity bring it home.

This is the most forceful argument for short courses upon the psychological and philosophical aspects of educational thought for the practising teacher. It is thus that the " rut " can be avoided and development sustained. It will be interesting to study the attitude of the more mature student of the emergency training college to this aspect of his work. Will his wider experience give depth to his thought, or will this be swamped by his need to refurbish his academic work? There are already indications that many of the teachers who have returned from the forces are bringing with them a critical frame of mind that is good to see. The teacher worth his salt is the one who realises that he does not " know all the answers," but has a sufficiently wide knowledge to realise what questions have to be asked.

CHAPTER IX

Teachers' Problems

The interest of the Secondary Modern School teacher should be focused primarily upon the child. This is desirable in all schools, but it is absolutely essential in this type of school. This does not mean that teachers should not be masters of the subjects they teach, nor that they should not be enthusiasts for their subjects. All this is important provided that all the time the primary aim of educating the children is kept to the front, and the aim of imparting knowledge and skill is regarded as a means to this end. This point has already been stressed in the previous chapter when it was suggested that specialisation should be limited so that the teacher could know intimately each child in his own class. It follows that the teacher should have a sufficiently wide knowledge of child psychology to enable him to set his study of individual children upon a sound foundation. Having gained an understanding of the needs and potentialities of his children, he must then be able to select and present his teaching material in the most effective manner. Since this again applies to all teaching, its special mention here signifies that such children need good, sound teaching, as opposed to chalk and talk.

PLANNING THE APPROACH

The key to success in teaching these children lies in the method of approach. It will be clear from what has been said earlier that there are three guides to the planning of this approach. First, if that drive which is essential to good work is to be attained, then the work which the children are asked to do must be sufficiently within their grasp, thus enabling them to succeed in achieving satisfactory results. Continual failure leads to frustration, and the barriers to progress thus set up can have very far reaching consequences both in work and conduct. It therefore follows that any teacher who finds that his lessons are not succeeding should not tell himself that it is because the children are lazy or stupid, but should examine his own methods. Children are not lazy, nor are they uninterested, if they are being presented with the right material in the right way. It is comparatively easy to teach bright children who will lap up whatever is put in front of them, but dull children really test the good teacher.

The second and third guides are both based upon our knowledge that these children do better in handling the concrete than the abstract. This is shown in the success that attends an approach which makes the fullest possible use of the practical and maintains its contact with reality. In such an approach the phrases, " Let us do this . . ." and " Let us go and see this . . ." will occur more frequently than, " Go and read it up. . . ." The implications of this approach have been discussed at length throughout the previous chapter, but its detailed application is a matter for each individual.

METHOD COPYING

In his " Education of a Community," Stead says (p. 139),

> " To imitate one pioneer because he or she has been successful in one set of circumstances is to misunderstand the nature of the problem of method. Method is the process by which the potentialities of the child are brought into contact with the situations in which they can be developed. In every situation the teacher is one element. The temperament and ability of the teacher affect the situation, and must be considered in connection with the other elements. To think that the situations are identical when teachers with different qualities are concerned is to fail to understand the root of the matter."

This does not mean that we cannot learn from a study of others' methods, for they can suggest many ideas to us, but we cannot hope to adopt them without interpretation. Each teacher must be an individualist, a creative artist with his own style and technique. To be successful he must possess two main qualities, enthusiasm and opportunism. While his first regard must be for the children, he will be greatly helped in his work if he is obviously an enthusiast. The master who is clearly keen upon local study and really knows his district, the music teacher who shows that he enjoys good music, the physical education man who is a keen athlete, all will find their enthusiasm spreading to the children; it is catching. To let your work become routine is both deadly dull for yourself and fatal for successful teaching.

To this enthusiasm must be added a sound opportunism. Opportunism has been too lightly treated in the past and thus has acquired a bad name. Some have advocated that almost every lesson should commence with the teacher asking the class what they would like to do, or encouraging them to ask questions so that upon these suggestions or queries the subsequent lesson can be built. This is opportunism carried to excess. But every teacher should be on the look-out for indications of interest which can be seized and developed. An item in the daily paper, a special piece of knowledge possessed by one of the boys in the class, a seemingly irrelevant point which crops up in a discussion, can often be turned to advantage. This does not mean that the work should sway this way and that with every passing whim but that when such indications appear the teacher should be ready to turn them to advantage. To do this he must know the material he handles and be for ever adding to this knowledge.

PERSONAL BIAS

Both of these considerations point to another important fact, often regarded as a failing rather than an asset, and certainly a failing if carried to excess. The field of every teacher's knowledge is bound to be biased by his own interests. Thus while one may be specially interested in History another may turn to Geography, Civics, Literature, or one of the Sciences. Thus it is natural that, although some balance in the core of the curriculum must be attempted in deference to the variety of the interests of the children, there will be a bias in the general attitude of the work. Local study for example can be approached from the historical, the geographical, or the scientific point of view, according to the special interests of the teacher.

Two other points regarding method need stressing. Visual and other aids to teaching are available today in ever growing number. Wall pictures, epidiascopes, film strip projectors and sound and silent films are of the greatest value in Secondary Modern Schools, for " seeing is believing " is very true of these children. But they must also understand. Professor M. D. Vernon, writing in the *British Journal of Psychology*, May 1946, shows that even simple symbolic representation of factual information is not understood unless it is taught. The child must be taught to look at pictures, films and diagrams. The work of G. P. Meredith, of the Visual Education Centre, University College of Exeter, on systematic visual education is arousing much interest, and it may lead to a new approach to the whole problem. School broadcasts can also prove of great value if properly handled. Every teacher should master the technique of the handling of these aids. That is, he should know how he can draw upon them to make his own teaching more effective. None of them will ever replace the direct contact between teacher and child, but each can serve to strengthen teaching power if carefully used.

The last point is a warning which every experienced teacher knows only too well. Even the best method wears thin in time, and there must be a constant search for something different. This is where the carefully planned Herbart lesson scheme broke down. It was an excellent scheme in itself, and fundamentally every lesson must be adequately planned, but it lost its appeal when applied too strictly in every lesson. Take another example. At one time there was a set of geography texts on the market which consisted of maps and questions upon them. The idea was that the child should answer the questions by reference to the maps and thus build up his knowledge of the subject. The idea was good—but not for a whole series of texts. Every other good ideas palls in the same way, so no method, however good, should be worked to death.

RECORD CARDS

The introduction of Record Cards to the schools both gives the teacher an added task and a great opportunity. In the Primary Schools the Record Card aids in the selection of the children for various types of Secondary School, and its aim is educational guidance. In the Secondary Schools, while it can still be of value for educational guidance during the school course, its cumulative evidence is of the greatest value in vocational guidance at the end of the child's school life. This is a matter in which the opinion of the various class teachers through whose hands the child has passed should be taken fully into consideration.

One of the difficulties of using the reports made by various teachers upon their children is that these tend to vary so from one individual teacher to another. First there is the problem of obtaining opinions upon those matters that are of real value. This is easily overcome by giving headings under which the report can be made. But the matter cannot be left there, for it is necessary to ensure that the implications of the headings are fully understood. This can be covered by simple explanations of the terms and of their grading. Then there is the difficulty of obtaining comparative estimates from a variety of teachers. Whereas one teacher will label the conduct of most of his class good, another will label most of his unruly, and so on. Much depends upon the attitude of the teacher himself. This difficulty is overcome by setting some guide to the proportion of children to be placed in each of the grades for one heading. Thus in the Secondary Record Card, published by the National Foundation for Educational Research, Perseverance is divided into :

A " Very persevering and tenacious."

B " Persistent in spite of difficulties."

C " Normal, persists until real difficulty arises."

D " Lacking in persistence, easily discouraged."

E " Easily distracted, very lacking in persistence."

Teachers are instructed to divide their pupils under these headings so that roughly 5 per cent are graded A or E, roughly 25 per cent B or D, and roughly 40 per cent C.

Although this may seem an artificial system, it is the only way in which comparative estimates can be obtained from a wide variety of teachers with any degree of accuracy. A full knowledge of the way in which such Record Cards work and a faithful completion of their items is one way in which the teacher can assist the guidance of his children in that initial choice of occupation which may mean so much to them in later life.

CHAPTER X

THE "EXTRA YEAR," AND THE SPIRIT OF THE SCHOOL

It is perhaps a pity that so much has been heard of the phrase, "The Extra Year." It has made it seem that this is a year which in some mystical manner stands apart from all other years. It is essential that we should think of the Secondary Modern School course as a whole; each year's work growing from the last. Thus, in speaking of the parts of the curriculum, each part has been considered as an entity, so there is no need for the curriculum of the final year to be discussed here. Yet each year in a child's life, whether at school or at home, is different from the others, and there are certain aspects of the age of 14 to 15 which are characteristic.

ADOLESCENCE

Most of the children of this age will be well into adolescence; not all, for adolescence is an individual matter just as is any other phrase of development. Too often the physical side of adolescence is stressed while its phsychological and social sides are ignored. Karl Mannheim, in *A Diagnosis of Our Time*, brings this out very clearly. The adolescent is essentially a seeker. He has left behind the temporary stability of later childhood and is feeling his way forward towards manhood. He is leaving the world of simple facts for one of ideas and ideals, and he has not yet acquired that sense of values and those standards of behaviour which will be a sign of his maturity. One of the main reasons for raising the school-leaving age is to enable the children of the future to plunge into the workaday world with more stable personalities than their less fortunate predecessors. The teacher can best help his children to find themselves by treating them as seekers.

The simplest way is to consider certain aspects of this questing. Many Secondary Modern School children seem, on the surface, to be hard-boiled materialists lacking both in enthusiasm and interest. One of the characteristics of the adolescent is that he becomes more introspective, and this cynical exterior usually conceals a sensitive and troubled real self. This real self cannot be expected to show itself in a crowd and often is still concealed even when contacts become more intimate. But upon occasions, and I can think of many in my own experience, we glimpse the underlying reality and must therefore cater for it all the time even though neither the need nor the results are directly apparent.

The main quest is fundamentally spiritual, for it is a search for a sense of values. All adolescents are religious, although their religion may vary from sheer superstition and sentimentality on the one hand to exalted mysticism on the other. We can provide children with the means to satisfy this need, not only through religious teaching, but by introducing them to the great and the beautiful in art, music and literature. A study of the actions and ideals of great leaders can also be of great help to them. Frank discussion with the children of their needs in these matters only scares them, but the teacher should be aware of his responsibility to provide for this need when he is planning his work.

On the more material plane the child is also seeking guidance for his future. He is frankly interested in things which will be of direct value to him in his work after school, but frequently he has no clear plan. This is partly because he is not aware of his own potentialities, and cannot be until he has tried his strength with the world, but also because he knows very little about this world itself. In a report upon the selection of children for Technical Education produced recently by the Association of Technical Institutions, stress is laid upon the need for a fuller introduction of children to the opportunities which life offers them. This is just as needful for the children of the Secondary Modern as of the Secondary Technical Schools. They should be taken about to see for themselves the work that is going on, and they should be given chances, both in school and outside, of meeting people in many walks of life. Devices such as the interviewing of workers in the school, which have already been described, can help in this.

LINKS WITH THE FUTURE

The linking of school life with work can be helped in the latter part of this last year by the development of the activities of the Juvenile Employment Bureau. If the officials of the Bureau are to know enough of the children to be of real assistance to them later, they need to make more contact with them, and, if these officials know their jobs, they should be the best people to assist in the introduction of the children to the wider world. Then again, it is to be hoped that most children will elect to join some youth organisation when they leave school, and facilities should be given for contacts to be made in this direction. Something is already done along these lines, but, as is shown by the comparatively poor response to the facilities offered, there are great possibilities for improvement.

Because he is a seeker after ideals, the adolescent is also a demander of the best. Whereas the adult will make allowances for deficiencies and make the best of what he is given, the adolescent does not do this. Short-comings he considers almost capital crimes, and he is quite intolerant when promises are not fulfilled and aims are not realised, whatever the reason. Those who succeed with adolescents know this and weigh their words and suit their actions accordingly. I well remember the case of a W.J.A.C. sergeant who, after her unit had been drilled by a R.A.F. Corporal, rated him soundly because he had not treated the matter sufficiently seriously. That is typical of the critical way in which the adolescent regards the fare prepared for him ; it must be the real thing and it must be well done.

Adolescents not only seek for ideals but they also are eager to try out their theories ; they are ready to assume responsibility. Naturally, this varies from individual to individual, but opportunities must be given to those who wish to try their new powers and to test themselves. A prefect system is valuable for this purpose, but there is no need here to expand upon the ways in which responsibility can be exercised by class and school organisation. A most interesting book which shed much light upon the problem of schoolboy responsibility is *Sane Schooling*, by J. H. Simpson.

The subject of the Extra Year cannot be left without mentioning A. Greenough's, *The Education of the 14–15 Age Group*, and *The Extra Year*, published by the A.E.C. and the N.U.T. The former fights fiercely for a free group system, but, unfortunately, does not explain the method in sufficient detail to make his suggestions really valuable ; the latter contains much that is both interesting and useful.

THE SPIRIT OF THE SCHOOL

We all know what we mean by the spirit of a school, yet it is difficult to describe or define it, and still more difficult to say how it can be fostered and developed. This is because it is a thing of the emotions rather than of the intellect. In this country we tend to ignore the emotions and yet these need as much education as the intellect. A great deal can be done by understanding the emotional development of children and working with the grain. This has been dealt with fully from the class teacher's point of view above, even though we have there been speaking especially of the older children, for it is these children who set the tone of the school. If they are right the rest will follow. But there are one or two points which affect the conduct of the school as a whole, and are therefore more the province of the Head than of the class teachers.

It has already been said that children are critical, but they are also proud. When things come up to their expectations they are stimulated by a pride in them to give whole-hearted support. A school in which things are done in an orderly manner, and in which high levels of conduct are expected, is more likely to evoke regard and support from its pupils than one in which anything will do. Just as classes do not like masters who let them do as they like, so children have no use or a school in which nothing really matters. Like all virtues, this can be carried to excess, in which case we have the old rigid system over again. The difference between the old and the new is that in the latter case the children are not passive, but are stimulated to an active response in support of the system.

The second point is closely allied to the first. Children like show. Hayward knew this when he produced his "celebrations," but he went too far. In the hands of a man of his calibre it was probably possible to take a concept like "liberty," to weave round it verse and music, to mount it in a theatrical manner, and so to effect an emotional change in his audience; but not everyone can do this. Most of us can play the tune better in a lower key. An effective and reverent assembly, a dignified prize-giving, a simple ceremony at the making of prefects or the presentation of school colours, a ceremonial welcoming of newcomers at the beginning of the year and parting with leavers at the end; all these can do much to set the tone of the school. They show that the Head considers them to be important matters and thus underlines them in the minds of the children.

Throughout these chapters stress has been laid upon the necessity to think out the problems of the Secondary Modern School from first principles. The first of these first principles is a knowledge of children. We started with this and we come back to it in the end. If we avoid the temptation to be led astray by academic tradition, by the memories of our own educational experiences (which more than likely are quite unsuited to the type of children with whom we have to deal), by subject teaching and specialisation, or by the desire to turn our children into encyclopædias, and if we base our efforts upon what we know of the children themselves, a new generation of schools will grow up which will really educate, in the fullest sense, these children of the Secondary Modern School.

INDEX

ACTIVITY, 36-7
Adolescence, 71-2, 73
Approach, 65-6
Arithmetic, 14-18, 25, 49, 55, 59, 60, 62
Art, 29-31, 49, 63
Assembly, 75
Attainment, 14, 59
Awareness, 37

BODE, B. H., 13
Brighton experiment, 37
British Journal of Psychology, 68
Broadcasts, 68
Burt, C., 35

CAMBERWELL, 49-51
Civics, 35, 48, 60
Child as individual, 10, 12, 26
Child and group, 12
Class organisation, 47
Classification, 14

DEMOCRACY, 9
Dewey, 36
Discussions, 56
Domestic Science, 26, 63
Drama, 32-3

EDUCATION ACT OF 1944, 9
Education for leisure, 31
English, 22-3, 63
Exhibitions, 46
Experience, 36
Expression, 22
Extra Year, 71

FACULTIES, 11
Fleming, C. M., 13

GEOGRAPHY, 35, 48, 60, 68
Geographical Association, 51
Grading, 59-62
Graphs, 46-7
Greenough, A., 74

HANDICRAFT, 63
Hayward, 75
Herbart, 68
History, 35, 48, 60

I. Q., 14
Individual work, 47-8
Information, 34, 35-6, 53
Intelligence, 59
Interest, 10, 28

JENKINS, J. W., 18

LOCAL STUDY, 39, 49-51, 66, 67
Look and say, 21

MANNHEIM, K., 71
Maps, 47
Mental Age, 14, 19
Metalwork, 27
Method copying, 66
Moray House, 18
Morrison, H. C., 13
Music, 31-2, 60, 63, 66

N. U. T., 74
National Foundation for Educational Research, 69
Needlework, 26
Non-verbal tests, 18

PHOTOGRAPHY, 47
Physical Education, 33-4, 60, 63 66
Pinsent, A., 13
Practical Subjects, 17, 24-8
Projects, 17, 38-52
Psychology, 11, 12
Purpose, 38-9

READ, H., 29
Reading, 19-22, 38, 55, 60
Record cards, 14, 59, 69-70
Religion, 72

SCHONELL, F., 15, 18, 19, 23
School journeys, 51

INDEX

School leaving age, 11
Science, 35, 48, 53-8, 63
Sentence Method, 21
Ship Adoption Society, 51
Simpson, J. H., 74
Social Studies, 35-52
Specialisation, 25, 62-4
Spelling, 22-3
Spirit of the School, 74-5
Standard Scores, 18
Stead, H. G., 13, 63, 66
Symbols, 46-7

TESTS. ARITHMETIC, 14, 15, 16, 18
" Intelligence, 14, 18, 19
" Reading, 14, 19

Time Tables, 48
Tool Subjects, 60

ULICH, R., 13
Utilitarian Appeal, 26-8

VERNON, M. D., 68
Visual Aids, 68
Vocational Appeal, 26-8, 72

WARMINGTON, N. V., 20
Woodwork, 27
Writing, 22

YOUTH ORGANISATIONS, 73